Best
Poetry

By
AZ Writers

Fogarty, Pat, ed. *Best Poetry* by Az Writers. Prescott. Granite Publishing October 2018. Print

ISBN 978-1-7328121-4-7

Granite Publishing
Prescott & Dover

9 8 7 6 5 4 3 2 1

First Edition

Printed in the United States of America
HBBXN 1551065906

Cover Design by Mariah Sinclair
Cover Photo by Cathy Severson

Preface

Best Poetry by AZ Writers is a perfect description of what you will find inside of this book. In this collection there are more than 50 well-crafted poems created by 25 established Poets. Each one contains a message for readers of all ages. On the pages of this collection, the reader will find a multi-faceted contemporary collection of poetry which includes Narrative, Epic, Free Verse, Haiku, Abstract, Sonnet, and more. These poems, by AZ Writers, are like wrapped-up gifts with a bow on top. Each one contains its own special message. And each poem is waiting for you, the reader, to unwrap it and discover its meaning. Sometimes the essence of a poem is obvious and sometimes you'll have to string the poet's words together and ponder a bit before you'll be able to find the true message of the poem. Enjoy.

Editor: Pat Fogarty

Acknowledgements

I would like to thank each and every Poet who contributed their fine work to help create this anthology of poems. Without their Dedication, Perseverance and Creative Talents, this book would not have been possible.

Preface	5
Acknowledgements	6
Goldie's Love	13
By Sherrie J. Lyons	13
Assault	15
By Brenda Whiteside	15
A Wedding in Connecticut	17
By James Raymond Thacher	17
Elegy for a Dying Planet	19
By David Nicoll	19
The Last Poet Writing	21
JamesRobert Platt	21
Chiropractor Engraving Scars on People's Backs	23
By Dan Dražen Mazur	23
Sweet Nothings	25
By James Raymond Thacher	25
Never More Soundly	27
By S. Resler Nelson	27
Untitled	29
By Sherrie J. Lyons	29
Paper Child	31
By Shirley Willis	31
The Cast	35
By Pat Fogarty	35
Friend	37
By Mike Doyle	37
Weather's Role	41
By Sherrie J. Lyons	41
Three Examples of English Haiku	43
By Mark Wenden	43
City Corn	45
By Pat Fogarty	45
Words for Robert Maillart	47
By S. Resler Nelson	47
Desert Night by Firelight	49
By Bruce D. Sparks	49
A Blessed Blizzard	51
By James Raymond Thacher	51

Portulaca	53
By Maureen Norcross	53
Hunting Turtles	55
By S. Resler Nelson	55
What is Love?	57
By Darlis Sailors	57
Temp's Lament	59
By Sherrie J. Lyons	59
Mia	61
By Susan Fogarty	61
Childs Play	63
By David Nicoll	63
Her Mom	65
By Pat Fogarty	65
Making Wine for Tryion Lannister	67
By Janice Shanks	67
The Wall	69
By Joe DiBuduo	69
My Maiden Aunt	71
By David Nicoll	71
Peonies	73
By Maureen Norcross	73
Virture of Verde	75
By C.L. Lynne	75
Tetter	77
By JamesRobert Platt	77
Time	81
By Susan Fogarty	81
So long, Tami	83
By Sherrie Lyons	83
Elegy for Modern Man	85
By S. Resler Nelson	85
Eclipse 2017	87
By Carol Bolinski	87
JamesRobert Platt	89
Poetry on the Runway	89
Baubles, Bangles and Beads	91
By David Nicoll	91

Greening of Holy Ground   93
By Dolores Comeaux-Everard   93
Dog Songs   95
By Carol Bolinski   95
Friendship   97
By Sherrie J. Lyons   97
Earth, Wind, And Fire   99
By C.L. Lynne   99
Beggar   101
By Elaine Jordan   101
Trying to Explain   103
By Bruce Paul   103
Ode to My Old Roman Nose   105
By Carolyn Jones   105
Ode to a Commode   107
By Dolores Comeaux-Everard   107
My Special Friend   109
By Kaya Kotzen   109
Cyberspace with Sleepytime Tea   111
By James Raymond Thacher   111
Tornado   113
By Carol Bolinski   113
Circles   115
Howard Gershkowitz   115
Newborn Foal   117
By S. Resler Nelson   117
Men   119
By Sherrie J. Lyons   119
Vaquero Solitario   121
By Bill Lynam   121
Unfit   123
By Joe DiBuduo   123
The Mole People   125
By Jude Crump   125
The Conductress   127
By Janice Shanks   127
Funky Friend   129
By Dolores Comeaux-Everard   129

Mad House   131
By James Raymond Thacher   131
Maria   133
By Bruce Paul   133
All Things Must Die   135
By Joe DiBuduo   135
Sherrie J. Lyons   137
So long, Tami   137
Heartbroken   139
By Bruce Paul   139
Summer Memories   141
By Pat Fogarty   141

Poetry is an echo,

asking a shadow to dance.

—*Carl Sandburg*

'If I read a book and it makes my body so cold no fire can ever warm me, I know that is poetry. Emily Dickinson

Goldie's Love
By Sherrie J. Lyons

Like a Down-syndrome child, who try as she might
Just doesn't comprehend,
You look trustingly into my watery eyes
Thinking that I'm your friend

But what kind of friend sends prayers up to God
Begging for you to die?
And what kind of friend takes steps on her own,
Ignoring God's reply?

The tears that I shed are not for you—
They selfishly roll for me
For you'll move on, but I must remain
With the truth you do not see:

I never truly loved you, dog
Though I walked and groomed you and such
For I saw you as a ditzy pooch
Who'd never amount to much

A retriever that wouldn't chase a ball
Or swim or even wade
And couldn't learn to speak or shake
Just didn't make the grade

Still, I would have found a place for you
To grow within my heart
If only you'd done that simple thing
That was keeping us apart

The iceberg that loomed in front of me
Was your passive attitude
You never smiled and wagged your tail
To show your gratitude

So I didn't see that your heart was pure
Loving children; strangers; all
And I didn't see your love for me
From behind that monstrous wall

But I see it now in your clouded eyes
Through my salty, raindrop tears
As the vet awaits my signal nod
To end your fifteen years

I stroke your head one final time
And turn to look away,
But a tiny flicker catches my eye—
And I curse this beastly day

*Dedicated to Goldie, age fourteen;
Not because it's true—but because it might have been . . .

Assault
By Brenda Whiteside

Being alone isn't so bad
Warm, cocooned in her bed.
She burrows deeper, chin tucked.
Satin-bound cover rests across her nose and cheeks.
Drawing her knees up to her chest, she tugs on her nightgown
Until even her toes are tucked, snug under flannel.
Night is quiet,
A veil of stillness.
Gossamer navy darkness.
The faint glow of moon drips from the bottom of the curtains.
Smiling into her pillow of night sensations, she surrenders to
                                            slumber.
Half-sleep dreams fill subsiding consciousness.
Then a sound,
Where none should be.
Eyes wide peer into shadows.
Dark scarcely melts, reluctant to reveal shapes of insipid hue.
Her breath catches on inhale.
She strains an ear on the void.
Her lips parted, body rigid.
The creak of the back-door hinge, then silence.
The deafening quiet drowns out her pounding heart.
Short gasps, clenching satin, crouched within covers,
She seeks more than warmth.
Impending footsteps,
Nameless intrusion looms.
Mouth dry, face hot, her chest aches from her pummeling
                                                heart.

She prays for invisibility, prays to be shadow in blackness.
Fear scrapes her throat, bathes her body in numbness.
She is no longer alone.

A poet can survive everything but a misprint.
—*Oscar Wilde*

A Wedding in Connecticut
By James Raymond Thacher

Has it already been
thirteen billion life years
since I've conceived this
image of you shimmering
walking down the aisle
of ten thousand universes
existing in an area as big as
a grain of sand held arm length out
in the pulsating hand of God
which is without a doubt
smaller and larger
taller and thinner
than anything I can perceive / than anything I can achieve
and can you believe / and two can believe
the size of that rock / this side of that rock
a diamond on a finger / door locked
your finger
touching mine
glowing in the dark of light
dressed in yellow
blessed in white
curtains drawn infinitely tight

Elegy for a Dying Planet
By David Nicoll

It may be inconvenient; the truth
And Al Gore's famous chart won't change some minds
For though his graphic rose to touch the roof
There's always those with attitudes enshrined.

The frozen North—the Pole—for what it's worth
Is now a summer route to distant shores
And snow-melt to the far side of the earth
Is quicker, cheaper passage than before.

Though icebergs break from ancient arctic sheets
And polar bears are stranded without snow
There's none so blind as those that will not see
Or deaf as those who do not want to know

Tornadoes blasting houses from their roofs
A swath of peoples' lives gets blown away
But climate change—though who could want for proof -
Is not the work of man, the skeptics say.

Records broken in the evening news
From New York City, down beyond The Keys,
Show hurricanes destroy familiar views
And most is lost by those who have the least.

Then California trembles as each shake
Could be the looked-for one that starts the fall
As earthquakes with Tsunamis in their wake
Show just how easily we lose it all.

We're faced with vital issues everywhere
And bumper-sticker wisdom says "Enough!"
As T-Shirts on a prudent group declare
"Don't trash the earth—it's where we keep our stuff!"

The sky is melting, shrinking, turning brown
And everywhere you look we're on the skids.
Our common global house is breaking down.
"Preserve the world—it's borrowed from our kids!"

Writing free verse is like playing tennis with the net down.
—*Robert Frost*

The Last Poet Writing
JamesRobert Platt

Do you write for yourself?
Do you write for others?
Do you write to reveal the truth
If not to seal your fate?
Do you write for publication
Stupefying an illiterate nation
Perhaps for personal gain
    To glorify your name?
Or is it to relive a past
When poems would last
Through the ages?
No need for pages
The ink of memory
Printing the images—the messages
On mental parchment
Not electronic
Without histrionics
    No clone poems
Neoteric poets labor to be different
By writing like other poets
The art finely mastered
In class
While sitting on your . . . mind!

The words
Have to be heard
In your voice
Valid poetry leaves no choice
For the last poet left writing
Must write in darkness
    And poets fear the light has already been turned off

'In my view a good poem is one in which the form of the verse and the joining of its parts seems light as a shallow river flowing over its sandy bed.'
—*Basho*

Chiropractor Engraving Scars on People's Backs
By Dan Dražen Mazur

I'd like to sigh my own air
And have my own precarity
If I was Hilary I would honestly reveal my sister's chest
So nobody would remember my scary face
I would try to look aside
So nobody would glimpse my eyes
If I was Hilary and a woman chiropractor
I would carve a long skinny scar on your back
So you will remember me by something else
And I would like to be seriously invisible
So nobody would have even a chance
To do bad things to me

Sweet Nothings
By James Raymond Thacher

As old as the ocean
Violin
This memory
I have
Of you
And the waves
Rolling in
On a vibrating
String
Of wind
And this
Thing
Called love
All Einstein
Eon
Sand
And science
Dissolving
In defiance
Reforming
The way weigh words
Written
On a fogged bathroom mirror
Are good
For remembering
Sweet nothings

Floating
On a stream
Of subconscious
Ionic
Extreme

'Like a piece of ice on a hot stove the poem must ride on its own melting.'
—Robert Frost

Never More Soundly
By S. Resler Nelson

Never more soundly will my lover sleep
Than this good night, wi th dark around his face.
If only his silence were half as deep
Then I might find some solace in this place.
For while the passing hours turn to late,
He stops, begins again, his hearty snore,
Which rises from a softened buzz, sedate,
And magnifies, vibrating to a roar.
Should I awake him with a sudden start
And bring this to a pause, if not an end?
Tomorrow yet complain to my sweetheart?
My right for nightly peace should I defend?
I more prefer his noise to muted breath,
Akin to separation and to death.

Untitled
By Sherrie J. Lyons

Where are you, John?
I look into your eyes, searching for something I can recognize,
But the man I loved is gone.

You stand there at attention, gazing down at me,
Your back as straight as it can be,
Saluting an unseen commander,
Reliving the life you loved the best.
And I sit here in my wheelchair,
Saluting you for a job well done,
But needing you to be here—in *my* reality.

I am old, John. *We* are old.
My body has forsaken me, as your mind has forsaken you.
I would have preferred the opposite to be true.
Seeing your mind disintegrate over time
Has been the most painful thing that I have ever endured.
And I have suffered much pain, John. And endured. And
endured.

Once, in another lifetime, we had each other,
And that was enough.
Now I am alone.
Even though you stand beside me,
You have abandoned me.
We vowed to stay together, "'til death do us part,"

But something worse than death has taken you from me.

I am tired, John. I am so tired.
I can no longer care for you,
And I no longer care for you.
You are not the man I loved.

Where is my John?
My John is gone.

Paper Child
By Shirley Willis

The paper child goes to Paper-Ruled School.
She sits in the corner, sorting paper cards at the little table, her
fingers long like a pianist, candle tapered.
She smiles her half-flirt, half-hurt smile.

The seven consultants consult at their big table,
coffee cups flashing,
pencils lashing,
their presentation smashing
for each other.
They can't say "retarded—retarded from birth."
They can say, "PDD/NOS,
Pervasive
Developmental
Delay
Not
Otherwise
Specified. PDD/NOS."

Her future is bleak, that child in the corner at the little table,
life compressed to initials.
She could be running.
Swinging.
Singing.
Touching blades of grass with candle-slim fingers.
Lighting the world with skyward smiles
Instead, she moves meaningless symbols where she won't
bother other learners.

At the big table by the window, the consultants seek words for
the non-verbal child—words for
parents
and peers.
"It's best," they say,
"for Sarah to sit, to sort colors,
to match numbers while we consult."

Sarah sits. Not bothering anyone but herself.
The consultants use reams of paper in order to not say retarded.
They only treasure
what can be measured—their shiny hubcaps of tiny
learnings

They count progress in decimals,
not seeing the child in corner who yearns to touch, to run .
Sarah's motor idles joy. Her fingers reach for data instead of
the real girl.

Sarah speaks.
No one hears.

The consultants squeak at each other and,
in their astuteness, they describe the child's muteness.
Their presentation shines
for each other.

The child soils herself.
Shifts in her chair.
That, the consultants hear.
They mark their charts.
The child has met the day's expectation.
Only one clothing change today.

Paper success. Paper child.

"Don't use the phone. People are never ready to answer it. Use poetry."

—Jack Kerouac

The Cast
By Pat Fogarty

Father, in our living room, I remember reading
"The Lady or The Tiger" to my siblings.
In our kitchen, mother inhales a deep breath
and wipes her brow with a worn dish towel.
Then, like magic she prepares a meal
fit for your majesty.

It's payday and you are late again.
The wall clock ticks away the minutes.
And panic, like a spreading virus, soaks the air.
A door slams and I keep reading.
You stagger towards the trail of my voice.
Your shoes pound like war drums.

Your little girls behave like frightened kittens.
They squiggle and squirm with no place to hide.
Your angry eyes stare and your daughters scatter.
Then, for no reason at all, you charge at me.

I tremble and wriggle as far away as I am able.
My arms rise over my head.
My legs pull up towards my small chest.
And, as your fist strikes my young knee,
I feel the punch and I hear your scream.

But, your broken hand and the agony in your face
delivers a strange comfort to my young mind.
And today, more than a half century later,
I still wonder
What did you tell your friends?

Friend
By Mike Doyle

I whispered your name as I awoke
I saw you in a dream
We were hiking up a mountain trail
Along an alpine stream.
The odd thing was
I wasn't sure
Just who you really were
And yet, I felt I knew you
From another place…
Sometime before.
I turned around,
looking down
To see where the water flowed
A sleepy hamlet down below
With stories…
yet untold.
I looked back up
And you were gone.
Where?
I didn't know.
And so I thought
Keep hiking on
to the source

of the waters flow.
It was a blissful place,
so serene,
Impossible to believe.
I felt I was
in a state of grace
I didn't want to leave.
And that was when
my big fat cat
Landed on my chest
As he leapt
from the windowsill
ME-owing
"feed me! get up! get dressed!"
Obedient cat-dad that I am,
I did as I was told.
Then I showered, shaved
On my way to work
Wondering
how my day would unfold.
I was sitting in traffic
Lost in my reverie,
Stitching together
Fragments of my dream.
Then the car behind me
honked its horn
The light had turned to green.
A gulp of coffee, NY strong
Jolted me awake
Now, armed and ready to right the wrongs
And to deal with the day's fate.
It's 5 O'clock

The work day's done,
I'm on my way back home
Suddenly, my dream
sprang back to life.
With a mind all its own
My head was flooded
with thoughts of you
as a wave washed over me
tossed and turned and upside down
very much like a tsunami.
And then it all became crystal clear.
I realized just who you were.
You are every friend
That I ever knew
Of that, I'm very sure.
You are Bryan, Diane, Carol D
Jimmy, Meg, Ray and Joe Ali.
A montage of faces
From distant places
alive within my brain
It's the memories of all of you
That helps to keep me sane.
Many of you are still here,
Some of you are long gone.
I hope that you
who have gone before
can guide us from beyond.
Just by being whom you are
Has made me rich beyond all measure
Yes, you are a guiding light
and your friendship
I will always treasure.

If perchance, when I dream tonight
I hope to find you
near that crystal stream.
And if I don't,
I'll again search tomorrow
In another realm of my dreams

.to all my friends with love, Mike

Weather's Role
By Sherrie J. Lyons

I want to be a millionaire
The gestating woman proclaimed on the air
'Orange' is the fruit with vitamin C
My final answer's decidedly 'D.'
And so, she continued to play the game
But the more she won, the less brash she became
'Haboob'? . . . 'Tsunami'? . . . I just don't know . . .
But I'm sure the answer is not 'Big Blow.'
I'd like to phone a friend of mine.
Sure, the host said, It's your last life-line.
Who's the friend you'd like to call?
Her name is 'Dot Com,'—she's a know-it-all.
Dottie, my friend, the question's on weather.
I hope that your mojo is all together.
By jinkies, Christine, our connection is bad
It's starting to sprinkle and thunder like mad.
I think we're in for a cyclone, my dear—
I'm sorry Christine—I simply can't hear.
'Cyclone' Dot said! That's letter 'A'
And good fortune shined on Christine that day.

Three Examples of English Haiku
By Mark Wenden

5-7-5 Syllabic Form

Haiku I

I cannot be lost
When all roads have the same name
I'm always right here.

Haiku II

≋

Silently speaking,
Unearthed ancients testify
Present will be past

Haiku III

≋

Hydrangea lovely
in rain, dream of a sun-kissed
moment before death.

"With me poetry has not been a purpose, but a passion."
—*Edgar Allan Poe*

City Corn
By Pat Fogarty

Carefully tap tap tapping in
time counting silent steps in
his mind a red tipped cane in
hand and hurrying to buy corn

While traffic horns blare in
ears tuned to scary sounds in
alleyways teeming with rats in
garbage chewing on rotten corn

In a ghetto of foreigners living in
a place where no one can speak in
his native tongue he stands mute in
serenity at a red-light corner for corn

Gentle hands petition his elbow in
gratitude he steps yet feels a sigh in
pity from this giving stranger who in
no way perceives of his quest for corn

Proves acceptance belies all faith in
others to shrink by an utterance in
foolish compassion for a man in
a rush to purchase perfect corn

With money he knows the sign in
a window states in six languages in
God we trust all others please pay in
cash and no checks permitted for corn

The man swings a white stick in
an arc intending to hit a hydrant in
front of his greengrocer his dealer in
an early summer harvest of sweet corn

An accented clerk places produce in
a canvas bag and says thank you in
English to a man tipping his hat in
reply and heads out with his corn

Home to a roach infested apartment in
a neighborhood with blind people in
every tenement watching others in
distrust without a handful of corn

From fire escapes stoops and roofs in
kitchen sinks tenement faucets leak in
soot filled ash cans along cellar walls in
tubs of rubbish rodents feast on dead corn

"Anon, who wrote so many poems without signing them, was often a woman."
—*Virginia Woolf*

Words for Robert Maillart
By S. Resler Nelson

Men with tethered minds never understood
your "puff-paste" bridges.

They never released themselves
to soar the precarious span between
two broken edges of the earth.

They never saw in those fragile concrete ribs
the flight of your restless spirit.

Desert Night by Firelight
By Bruce D. Sparks

Old wood we found in a wash, good for nothing but burnin'
Let's drag some in 'n make us a fire, start some old stories a
churnin'

Friends and family all gathered 'round, feel alive as the embers
glisten
Wind dies down but the fire burns on, and stories too good not to
listen

Parts of our lives from a bygone age, kindled like old wash wood
Chilly winter night yet warm by fire's glow, times and tales so
good

Put on another piece of old wood to burn, get us a blaze a goin'
Stir up those coals a bit, old pard, old wood and stories a glowin'

Tell a tall tale but don't you dare lie, we know the truth when we
hear it
We want to be taken away for a while, stretch it and make us
believe it

Cold desert night with a fire for our light, good food, good drink
and good friends
Here we share the joys of the hunt, before the night comes to an
end

These are good times that will end one day, we all have that for
the learnin'
Gone soon the stories to tell 'round the fire, like the old wash
wood we are burnin'

A Blessed Blizzard
By James Raymond Thacher

Amounts to eighteen inches.
A silent white.
Born of hellish night.

Zero viability driving.
At one a.m. on the highway home.
Crawling along, following a plow truck.

High wind makes of icy flake a plague of locust.
Nothing left to waste by ravage.
Even the radio waves are eaten.

Only the plow truck dome light orange.
Breaks through at a haphazard pace.
Then every now and then red emergency flasher.
A tap on the brake, to keep me thirty feet back, give take.

To finally veer right on the exit ramp.
Post Road more of a ghost road.
I a stranger in a strange land.
Coming in from Los Angel-ease.

Following the plan the plow truck stops.
The burly driver gets out and tucks in.
Points a right hand finger towards the rectory.
And this is where it all begins. The end.
Of a woman on a mission. In a sea of tranquility.

Happiness radiates like the fragrance from a flower and draws all
good things towards you.
—Maharishi Mahesh Yogi

Portulaca
By Maureen Norcross

she gathered us when
we were full of the future
saving for another season
to greet all
with exclamation of life
receiving with sweet smiles
we take our time
we are tiny seeds
with aspirations
to glow with blooms
exploding with fanfare
to greet your eyes
for another season of color

we are planted with watchful eyes
we are tendered with care
we send forth our flowers
till it's time to gather once again.

Hunting Turtles
By S. Resler Nelson

Beneath overhanging ledges of foliage
And unclear rippling of clear water,
Turtles hide in muskrat caves.

My brother and I,
With long hooked poles,
Like blind men, feel the dark river banks.

My pole thuds against a log,
Heavy and solid,
Then cracks
On the turtle with the bounce of a ripe watermelon.

I snag his shell and pull his clawing body
Into the sun.
His head rolls, snapping the air as if he knew
About the dark, musty barrel on the back porch...

Where he'll be kept alive
On buttermilk and flies until the junkman
(Who deals in various other things)
Comes to buy our catch.

What is Love?
By Darlis Sailors

LOVE is fragile,
Like a flower in bloom.
Nurture it carefully,
Let it grow.

LOVE is challenging,
Like a trail in the woods.
Explore it slowly,
Discover its joy.

LOVE is valuable,
Worth effort and time.
Invest it thoughtfully,
Reap the rewards.

LOVE is emotional,
Up, down, twirled around.
Buckle your seatbelt,
Risk the ride.

LOVE is sharing,
Both laughter and tears.
Open your heart,
Widen your world

"Poetry is when an emotion has found its thought and the thought has found words." – Robert Frost

Temp's Lament
By Sherrie J. Lyons

Consigned as relief to understaffed places
Prepared to change jobs on a daily basis
You try to look and perform your best
Outwardly smiling, inwardly stressed

Wherever the job, it's always the same
Your badge bears a number—never your name
Your training consists of one or two tries
The desk you're assigned has been stripped of supplies

The copy machine is an albatross
When questions arise, you can't find your boss
You can only make calls from a special phone
And when lunchtime arrives, you eat alone

As the days wear on, you start to fit in
You're thankful not to move on again
But you're barred from training, meetings, reviews—
You're always the last to hear vital news

Then after weeks of working late
Just when you think things are going great
Down comes the final indignity
The ultimate corporate malignity

Of being "released" with no explanation

No handshake, no "thank you," no personalization
Disposed of like trash thrown out on the street
You take a day off to climb back on your feet

Then ignoring foreknowledge of what to expect
And suppressing the pain of lost self-respect
You move on to another similar place
Recycled again, with that same smiling face

The life of the dead is placed in the memory of the living.
—Marcus Tullius Cicero

Mia
By Susan Fogarty

You were . . .
The sole redhead to capture my heart
Who knew you would leave me so soon
You were my shadow and comfort
At times of stress or sadness
On that dark day we said goodbye
Emptiness filled my heart
Tears flowed like a dam had broken
Part of me went with you
The moment you crossed over
The Rainbow Bridge

"Poetry is the spontaneous overflow of powerful feelings: it takes its origin from emotion recollected in tranquility."
—William Wordsworth

Childs Play
By David Nicoll

Provide a child a box of bricks
And see him make a pile
Then hear him chuckle as he makes
His pyramid collapse and break
And clatter on the tile.

Give a child a rubber ball
To throw across the floor.
He laughs with glee at once because
A throw which uses little force
Comes bounding off the wall.

Observe a boy with stones and rocks
In some neglected place.
He picks a grimy window-frame
And takes it out with just one aim -
To leave an empty space.

And thus it goes from boys to men
The pleasure's still the same.
A pyramid of empty cans,
And bottles broken in the sand,
Upon the desert range.

Or later, shooting at the club
He practices his skill
The most effective way he can
Destroy the outline of a man
If he has need to kill.

Give a man a gun that fires …
Five shots a second should suffice …
To fill the empty outline in
And decimate a human life.

To chuckle as they hit the floor
Delighted that such little force
Will knock them down and leave their lives
In pieces on the floor

Her Mom
By Pat Fogarty

On Sundays cluttered halls
play host to warm metal meal bins
sitting idle while vile
canvas laundry baskets vex
harried nurses pushing locked
narcotic carts stocked to
sedate strident clients who
behave like craving addicts

That Sunday her mom leaves
with my bride holding the hand
that wiped her childhood tears
and walked her to school
and punished and protected
and was all that mattered
to the daughter who could not
let go of the woman she lost

That Sunday my words fell
like futile bombs on numb
ears that shutout the muttering
promises of a well meaning
groom who like a callous fool
begged his bride to refrain and
to compose and to be calm and
to cease her niggling babble

This Sunday at Serenity Hills
another daughter weeps and
another daughter begs and
another daughter prays and
another daughter pleads and
another daughter cries for
a mother whose love and loss
will sear her heart forever

Making Wine for Tryion Lannister
By Janice Shanks

These are flora,
fragrant grapes,
minuscule purple, black as a bruised eye.
Small grapes, ripe, a vintage for a tiny man with large hands.
My small hands pluck each blue berry off its stem
and drop each broken skinned orb
into the wooden barrel,
sending up a rare perfume.
This task is endless,
plucking each bead on the rosary,
revealing spring green pulp,
leaving stained fingertips, inked cuticles, pruned skin.
Lifting another bunch from the vat,
nimble fingers journey up the river of amaranthine nectar,
working each bunch of prayers,
breathing violets and cloves.
Small hands roll grapes off the stems,
fermenting in seconds.
In yonder times Tyrion drank
this rich magenta wine
to excess.
Large hands cupped his goblet.
Tiny man had his fill,
then sought revenge after the drunkenness,
killed his own,
and took up his manly journey.
Broken and sober
he now seeks his allies clearheaded,

shrugging the haze of waste.
As I perch on a lowly stool,
plucking,
thinking of him unleashed,
I wonder
what alliances,
what strength and power,
what courage will this valiant prince
allow himself?
Will he, the victor, sit on the Iron Throne
drinking my vintage?
Dare he lift the chalice
to honor my people?

"Cannibals prefer those who have no spines."
—*Stanislaw Jerzy Lec*

The Wall
By Joe DiBuduo

I have learned sharks can live for four hundred years or more.
It
appears turtles live that long too, unlike humans who can't see
any light after a hundred years have passed. I must ask
"Why?"

Why, we have to die so soon? I don't have a clue why other
creatures
live so many more years than we? I become afraid and scared
when I
think about going through death's door. If I have a soul, where
will it go?

What will I owe after all the years I've been here? There are so
many worlds
out there that I like to believe we're here to train how to
behave on the one
we'll go to when our spirit leaves our body here and ascends
up there.

After we meet our end, will I comprehend, or twiddle my
thumbs for fun while I
wait my turn for my soul to soar up to a planet chosen for me
by the one

who sent me to live here? Once I go, I'll become an alien like
him.

It's true; I believe God is an alien being, unlike you and me
who are never free.
Where God came from, no one knows, but many suppose and
believe what
the scriptures say, "God was here before the moon and stars."

God created Earth and everything in it, but he wasn't born in
the USA, or anywhere
else on this world, so If I happen to see God, should I call the
police or ask for his
green card because he's the one alien the wall can't keep out?

My Maiden Aunt
By David Nicoll

Oh Lord, please let me not grow old the way my maiden aunt has done;
Her bitterness is uncontrolled—she takes it out on everyone;
And though she needs a helping hand to get her through her every day
She doesn't seem to understand she's driving everyone away.

Finding fault is her domain and she will likely misconstrue
My actions, and then she'll complain of every little thing I do.
My patience tried, I bite my tongue and contemplate what made her thus
Just what went wrong when she was young that made her so cantankerous?

Sometimes I think that it must be because she can't control her life
She focuses on little needs and turns them into daily strife
Making helpers want to leave. So it's so hard to comprehend—
Despite the treatment we receive we keep on to the bitter end!

Oh Lord, my maiden aunt has died—I should be glad that she has gone.
I know in every way I tried to ease her life e'er she passed on.
It was not fun and by the end, while there's no need to wonder why,
She lost the chance to be my friend—a thing for her in scarce supply.

It seems to me when we depend upon another for our needs
It's better not to mar our end by biting off the hand that feeds!
I grieve that she has passed away and wonder why it matters so
But it is such a subtle grade, the line twixt love and duty owed!

"He is happiest who hath power to gather wisdom from a flower."
—Mary Howitt

Peonies
By Maureen Norcross

white with a strike
of dark wine
dashing through
the snowball

heavenly
fragrance
feathered with
angel kisses

'Poetry is the journal of a sea animal living on land, wanting to fly in the air.'
—*Carl Sandburg*

Virture of Verde
By C.L. Lynne

Land of freshness
vast and blessed,
where junction of
earth and sky surround

Small brush on
gentle inclines—
a winding highway
leads to iron profusions

Where roundabouts and
populous now preside,
yet beauty speaks
and thrives

Since nothing manifest
from man
can ever override
this pure domain.

Tetter
By JamesRobert Platt

Voicemail beckoned. I listened to the
message from my little sister, her love and
best wishes to one and all. And then the news,
the news she knew I would sadly need to hear:
"Jim Tetter has died."
A brief, brave, cancer battle ending just a few days
past Christmas, before the rest of us celebrated a
fresh start, time's annual rebirth. My niece and Jim's
daughter are friends, another bond from adolescence.
Without pause, I phoned my youngest sibling.

I last saw Jim when I attended the Junior Miss Pageant
at our old high school. A wonderful program which
showcased the talents of Jim's daughter and my niece.
I spotted him on the stage after the final curtain,
embracing and praising his child. A proud father,
happy husband . . . and rightfully so. Climbing
the stairs, I walked toward him with extended hand,
calling his name and announcing mine, re-introducing
myself across the aged planks, decades of separation.
Smiles, congratulations, small talk,
brief reminiscences, and laughter.
The handshake goodbye.

Living on the opposite side of the continent, I never saw,
nor spoke to, Jim again. My sister's words awakened
the memories of youth; both of us stirred to melancholy.
He was a frequent visitor, in and out, going through our

parents' house. I winced, certain I felt the body aches
we long ago inflicted on each other, playing tackle football
on the perfectly manicured grass of Green's Farm. When
he got wheels, I hitched rides with him to school, sharing
early morning glee club, history, English, study hall, and
last-period music class. Jim advancing above my poor
trumpeting to become the master tuba/sousaphone player
of the high school marching band.

Graduation.

Each life's road veering its own course.

He stayed rooted; I became a vagabond. Jim hired me
once as a summertime security guard at the local department
store. A generous gesture to a struggling college friend
by the up-and-coming assistant manager. Later, boots on,
he served. The army, Korea, eventually returning to family
and finding his place, pleasure, and career, completing his
appointed rounds for the Post Office in our hometown.

I headed west.

Today, my sister's call, her heart draped at the outset.
The holidays had brought the loss of her dear cat, "Biscuit."
An abandoned tabby kitten she rescued from the dumpster
near her office, more than fourteen years ago. Jim's passing
encircled tearful days. And yet, this season also gave my sister
the joy of grandchildren, being able to steal their magic.

Somehow there is balance.

As we talked, my thoughts rewound to New York City. Not
the traditional wild New Year's Eve celebration, but the
Easter vacation taken by two seventeen-year-old schoolboys,
alone–no chaperon. My first plane trip was to the Big Apple.

My first hotel stay and skyscraper elevator ride were in
Manhattan. My first visit atop the Empire State Building, the

Statue of Liberty, the sidewalks of Times Square, and my only
tour
negotiating the corridors and assembly hall of the United
Nations.
Two teenagers sitting in a studio audience watching the
filming
of Allen Funt's (and Durward Kirby's) television show,
impatiently
waiting for the TV camera to scan our faces and hear Allen
shout:
"Smile, you're on Candid Camera!"

The first great adventure of my life.
Jim Tetter and I.
No reservations, no concrete plans. Too young to get into
the bars, and into trouble. That is why my father said yes
over my mother's protests. That is why a couple of small-town
boys returned conquering heroes with exaggerated tales and
gaudy Batman ties. A feat unmatched even by our school's
elite–
the athletes, the cheerleaders, the moneyed, and the in-crowd
Me and Jim.
A memory that has survived a lifetime and binds me to him
now,
and forever. Jim, you helped set in motion the urge to travel,
to move about, to explore and experience beyond our
backyard.
To try new things despite fear, and often common sense.
You were there when a door opened, and I would not let it
close.

Thank you, friend. Godspeed.

lost years find comfort
knowing kindness defies death—
good deeds (and men) last

Time is a fluid condition which has no existence except in the momentary avatars of individual people. There is no such thing as was—only is
—William Faulkner

Time
By Susan Fogarty

Our Past
Never returns
Our Today
Never leaves
Our Tomorrow
Never comes
Our Eternity
Never ends

"Friendship is born at that moment when one person says to another: 'What! You too? I thought I was the only one."
—*C.S. Lewis*

So long, Tami
By Sherrie Lyons

So long as you are alive
I want to be part of your life:
To chat with you over the phone
To sit with you alone—or not—
In a car or at a restaurant
At my house or at a park
Anywhere your spark
Flames or flickers or faintly glows
Because my heart knows
That your life fuels my life.

The smile in your voice brightens my day
Your sunny spirit shows me a way
To live my life better
And whether or not I achieve this end
I can't thank you enough for being my friend
For so long, Tami—forty years or more—
And no matter what life holds in store
I'll always feel blessed
Because you possess
A warmth that can't pass away.

Dedicated to Tami Knapp (1959-2017)

I do not want people to be very agreeable, as it saves me the trouble of liking them a great deal."
—Jane Austen

Elegy for Modern Man
By S. Resler Nelson

Here lies 13978M3110
Programmed 1970 in
Trenton, New Jersey.

While passing through the
Processing Machine of Life,
He was stamped,
Folded, mutilated,
And rejected in triplicate
On May 19, 2046.

And by the way, everything in life is writable about if you have the outgoing guts to do it, and the imagination to improvise. The worst enemy to creativity is self-doubt.
 —Sylvia Plath

Eclipse 2017
By Carol Bolinski

It was so brief
so fast
so very very far away

walking on half moons
the anticipation more exciting
than the actual event

but after the darkness
a sliver of light
beamed some hope, that
the world would be right again

JamesRobert Platt
Poetry on the Runway

The prestigious literary review announced its upcoming literature festival, and promoted a featured author's scheduled appearance and credentials: *Poet, Instagram star and model.*

Once upon a time we saw Hollywood stars, TV stars, and sports' stars; some folks long ago amazingly looked to the heavens to find stars. Apparently, our star search has become unlimited, and less intense. Stars are discovered and declared everywhere (far too many being self-proclaimed). Now we have Reality Show stars (let's keep on script, please), Op-ed Talking Head stars (making me believe in fake news), YouTube stars, Twitter stars, and not to be ignored or under-marketed— Instagram stars.

Exactly how trite has stardom become? Is there no longer a need, a place, for simple hardcopy poetry publication, paying your dues, or possibly learning to write (excuse me, tweet) using more than 140 or 280 characters? How about having to actually "pen" a lyric line? Today, would Emily Dickinson, Robert Frost, e. e. cummings, and Sylvia Plath be texting while catwalking a fashion runway, followed by posting original poetic compositions (plus photos, of course) on their websites and blogs? Is the look or the book what's important?

It must be the number of "friends" and "hits" that matters; or is it the number of friends you hit? (Poetry should always come at you hard!) My cynicism is probably unfair. Yes Heraclitus, I know, change is the only constant. It's just that the writers that I respect, read, and purchase, describe themselves as poets— period. Any resume embellishments may include novelist, playwright, storyteller, activist, teacher, student, parent, or anarchist. Not celebrity; not star. Clearly, my own social-networking aptitude was sidestepped at the passing of the previous century. Perhaps there actually was a Y2K millennium bug. (I do vaguely remember feeling somewhat ill on New Year's Day 2000.)

My rambling discourse leaves me wondering if even I could become a world-renowned star (I mean poet). But I'm left to ponder how much weight my work might really have. A gram? (Which equals 0.035274 ounce.) Upon reviewing my poetry (and my looks), maybe a gram is fitting for a star that truly would shine only for an instant.

Poetry is language at its most distilled and most powerful
—Rita Dove

Baubles, Bangles and Beads
By David Nicoll

In the Sahara the desert is bare -
It's a most inhospitable land.
Arabia too has no water to spare -
It's devoid of all substance but sand.
Through ages uncounted the bactrians plod
Down the trade routes where Bedouin drivers have trod
In a long slow procession with satins and silks
And perfumes and spices and coconut milk.
For the merchants and camels with such caravans
Must ferry them over the sands.

A desert is not a secure place to dwell
Not even for people who cross it twice yearly
And after successfully growing his wealth
By trekking across the Rub al-Kha'ili
He changes his goods into silver and gold
Which he hides in his clothing by strengthening hems
And stitching false pockets to hide and to hold
The rest of his fortune in jewelry and gems.
No bank for deposits; no safe box to rent
For keeping the profit he's made.
A prosperous merchant who wants to remain
Must use such devices so he can retain
The spoils of his toil and his trade.

How else must a prosperous merchant be clad
To protect his estate from the thieves of Baghdad?
He fashions the metals as things one can wear
Like ringlets and breast plates and clasps for the hair
To present to the women (of which he has four)
All wearing silk dresses (that reach to the floor)
Beneath their abayas (with slits for their eyes)
They wear golden ornaments 'proud as a prize'.
With a line of gold bangles from elbow to wrist
Which mostly they jangle, they twirl and they twist
And compete with their wealth for the others to see
Just "how much our husband cares more - about ME".

Greening of Holy Ground
By Dolores Comeaux-Everard

Dear Spirit, Sweet Spirit,
Forgive us our trespasses,
For repeatedly we forget
How lovingly you nurture
And care for your creations.

Dear Creator, Sweet Source,
Has adorned us with splendor
And plenty for Life's playground,
A plethora of pleasure for humanly delights.

Pathetic, bulimic beaches are strewn with plastic,
And city sidewalks are dotted with dog-doo,
While grassy byways are bombarded with cigarette butts
From forgetful wayfarers, revelers, and residents.

Dear Spirit, Sweet Spirit,
Forgive us our trespasses,
Lead us not into litter
But deliver us from
Daily destruction of our inheritance.

I hide in a corner wrapped 'round in a curtain,
For I have forgotten to stand on a soapbox
Proclaiming the Principle
That wherever we stand is Holy Ground.

Dear Spirit, Sweet Spirit,
Empower us immediately
To cleanup your Kingdom
Forever and forever. Amen.

"Until one has loved an animal, a part of one's soul remains unawakened."
–Anatole France.

Dog Songs
By Carol Bolinski

The songs that pour
from your young throat
between new teeth
and vocal cords you're
probably trying out
The sound of throat
rasping breath
rejoicing or warning
Those special doggy sounds
the ones that playfully call out to your brother
and end with nips to your ears
The ones that cautions and
the ones that whine because
you want to go outside or
have more to eat
or want a hand for affection
The tones that excite question
ask and plead
The sounds that make others say
Why does your dog bark so much

It's interesting that I understand
more from you than I do him

Him and I who speak the same
language the same idioms
and have the same vocabulary
Is it because I want to understand
what you want
what you need
what you try to sing to me
Is it because I love you more
than him
Or is it that I'll never be sure

Friendship
By Sherrie J. Lyons

I can no longer be your fan.
It is too degrading.

With my spouse
and siblings
and friends,
I am an equal.

With you,
I am a dog,
eagerly awaiting
a pat
or friendly word
or even a kick in the ribs.

A dog is man's best friend.
But you are not seeking friends.

Perhaps,
someday,
you will be.

Then,
when a fan gives you
a roll of Lifesavers,
you will know to offer her
the first piece of candy.

'Poetry is the record of the best and happiest moments of the happiest and best minds.'
—*Percy Bysshe Shelley*

Earth, Wind, And Fire
By C.L. Lynne

Sputtering jolts disrupt a day
where calm began.
Windows rattle, shelving shakes—
Treasures fall and figurines break

Hearts beat faster;
dishes tremble
pulsating ground, machine-gun sound.
Land rebelling, land releasing

Calm again where gentle wafts of air
distinct as branches sway
with leaves a jiggle,
Whoosh and wiggle.
Zephyrs ascend

until drifts of smoke emerge
from orange glow, crackling flames
flurry and grow
to burning furor—

Consuming brush and dry debris
into rhythmic inferno, diminishing
upon hydration and chemical warfare.
Rage is overpowered in defeat.

*'Poetry isn't a profession, it's a way of life. It's an empty basket;
you put your life into it and make something out of that.'*
–Mary Oliver

Beggar
By Elaine Jordan

His hand extends
For a coin
A veteran
Head shaved
Stalks me
Among candies
And toasted corn
In the Juarez market
His American eyes
Raging
At my prosperity.

Combat boots drum
Entreaties
Spilling succulence
Ripe with nothing
I need.
He shouts
I hope
You'll find yourself here
Some day
A curse from Hell
For a Christian tourist.

Frantic guitar
Blasts of brass
Mock my scurry
A guilty lizard
Hiding between stalls
Safe behind
Piles of golden mangos
Mounds of chilies
Baby iguanas tied with ropes.

Acrid odor of urine
Drenches my heart
While Jesus
Begs for deliverance
With desperate hand.

Poetry doesn't belong to those who write it, but to those who need it.
—Unknown Source

Trying to Explain
By Bruce Paul

Standing on a highway,
Riding on a train,
Trying to understand,
Trying to explain.
There are many ways to be alone.
Listen to the wind whisper and moan.

A crazy riddle:
The windowpane—
Caught in the middle—
Was broken in vain.
There are many ways to be alone.
Listen to the wind whisper and moan.

The man in the moon
And I never know
Why some die,
Why some grow.
Lost in the moment,
We find what we need,
And—truth or lie—
We plant every seed.

I stood on a highway,
She rode on a train,
Unable to understand,
Unable to explain.
There are many ways to be alone.
Listen to the wind whisper and moan.

Ode to My Old Roman Nose
By Carolyn Jones

As far as I know
all humans have noses. We use them to smell garlic and roses.
Essential to breathe, fresh air is the best—
no pollutants to clog one's nose or chest.
Tempting it may be
to see what can fit in those tiny chambers just north of the lip.
Neither BB's nor peas nor Halloween candy
should be stored in your nose, no matter how handy.
Told not to pick it—
you secretly do, in lots of places you think out of view.
But it's better to blow, and please use a hanky!
They come in all colors, some rather swanky.
Bugs flying about,
without detection, can enter the nose—lead to infection.
You try every cure bandied about,
including the ones you snort up your snout.
Your poor schnoz reddens—
it doubles in size. It throbs when you blow and you agonize.
With tissues nearby, you dab every drop
and wonder aloud, *Will this ever stop?*
Straight-edged or sloping,
bent like a ski-jump. Flat as a pancake—reshaped by a fist-bump.
Beak-like or bulbous, fleshy or pointed,
no matter its shape, we're STILL disappointed!
Cyrano once thought
his nose a real blight. He feared the ladies would not treat him
right

Cursed with that honker, he didn't pursue
the lovely Roxanne he wanted to woo.
Standards of beauty
change over time; a hook in one's bill was once thought sublime.
But these days you're teased…as happened to me,
so I changed my look with rhinoplasty.
The irony is
I now understand, my old Roman nose was really quite grand—
and beauty that's of the physical kind—
it's soon surpassed by one's spirit and mind.
So, friend if you have
a nose that's freaky, it's better than one that's always leaky.
Remind those who jest, and poke fun at you,
what's given is got…goes right back…*ah-choo!*

"Poetry is a way of taking life by the throat."
—Robert Frost

Ode to a Commode
By Dolores Comeaux-Everard

The imprint of a toilet lid
Indelible as ink on my butt;
The lower half of my body
Perched precariously on the seat;
Explosion of tidal waves of toxins
Spew like a rampaging faucet into the bowl.
    Then
Blast! Splash! Plop. Flush,
Throd-a-throd,
Hummm...

Sings the slush that slaps the toilet water,
An ode to the commode commences:
Minute after minute,
Hour after hour,
Prep for the poop shoot snoop
Marches on and on.
    Then
Blast! Splash! Plop. Flush.
Throd-a-throd
Hummm...

The stomach clinches a last time;
Stillness sooths the muscle contractions,
All is calm- all is quiet
Like the eye of the hurricane.
Peace prevails and squatting ends;
Stand and collapse to beach towels strewn on the floor.

The first hurdle produces weakness and whining;
The clean-out for sure is *merde.*
Debris dumped and liquid clear,
Until the morning light: another round.
Slugging back a gagging cocktail to explode,
Making a mad dash to the throne of terror.
    Then
Blast! Splash! Plop! Flush.
Throd-a-throd
Hummm...

Just for the health of it,
My backside heaves and rattles.
Bugle butt and thunder rump
Storm the commode in a *blitzkrieg.*
Propped against the wall for strength,
Hoping for a cease fire from my nuclear derriere.
    Then
Fine. Silence. Peace.
It's over, thanks be to God.

The privilege of a lifetime is being who you are.
—*Joseph Campbell*

My Special Friend
By Kaya Kotzen

I want the wind to carry me out into the universe when I'm gone.
I want it to blow my ashes around mountains and into streams.
I want it to sweep me inside of the base of a mesquite tree
and up into its center so that I could be part of the dancing
branches
that I always see, that are so very magical to me.

I want the freedom of the wind to blow my restlessness away,
to carry my fear away from my being along with any doubts.
I want it to blow me across oceans and to
hold up the planes that I ride in while I cross the vastness of
countries that I long to see.

I want my writing to flow like the wind across the page with
no punctuation or capital letters.
I want to not care how it looks, only how it sounds.
I want the wind to breathe words into my soul for the things
I don't have language for yet so that I can share them all.

I want to discover and uncover so much of the world I have not
yet seen.
Would that the wind could levitate my body when I become tired
or my legs and feet sore that I can still carry on.

I ask the wind not to blow chairs off my porch or damage my
home
while I'm gone, this summer, but rather be like an aura of
protection around it,
swirling gently and lovingly to protect it from storms and heat.

I would ride the wind like a stallion if I could,
saddled and holding on to the horn for dear life
as it galloped through the sand.
Like the whale rider, I would become one with it
and trust where it took me into places unknown

The wind is a woman,
constantly changing, softly caressing, and
carrying me forward in this life.
I want her to hold me up as my body ages and let the feel of her
remind me of when I was once young without a care in the world,
with grasshoppers for daily pets,
remembering the time when I'd find lightening bugs in the dark
at nite,
when fears of the forbidden and strangers
had yet to be thrust into my face,
causing me to both wonder and rebel at the world I lived in.

The wind blows away worries, and welcomes my dreams,
supports my intuition, and embraces me when I need her
in the dark of the early morning when I walk my dog.

The wind is a gift and a welcome friend.
I invite her to be a part of all my days.

Cyberspace with Sleepytime Tea
By James Raymond Thacher

I'm tired of contemplating
Myself
This Earth
Those stars
The universe
Accelerations
Spinning in my head
Intergalactically wired into
You
And everything
We have been through
As beings do
I'm tired
In reverse
Crickets
Peep toads
Highway traffic
Buzzing by
Across the Magellanic sky
My meandering eye
Driving fast forward
In hypothetical statement
Imperatives in a net
Compromised
Of categorical probabilities
Commanding
I close my mind

Shut down
Go to sleep
As I am bound
To do
Not in weakness
Not in strength

In fact
That I am
Wired
Intergalactically
Into you

'Poetry is the music of being human.'
–Carol Anne Duffy

Tornado
By Carol Bolinski

Its bad tempered fingers
reach out, whip
counterclockwise,
then knead the earth
twirl it around
and drop debris
into the hands
of prayer.

Circles
Howard Gershkowitz

An elm stood here once;
branches supported a 360 sky,
and birds' nests hidden in crannies
protected by cut glass curtains of leaves.

Roots, spread like ant tunnels
deep in the soil,
delivered life giving nutrients
through bark shielded veins.

Season upon season,
year after year,
rings captured their passing
on its own parchment skin.

Now, a grey stump remains;
a footprint of circles
telling the story, marking the ages
from seed to stalk, vibrant to vanished.

Standing upon it, gazing aloft,
I sense its vitality
as stars circumnavigate
above me and wonder;

As my own circles darken,
and my roots grow wrinkled and dry,
who will stand on the trunk I leave behind,
and count the rings?

Newborn Foal
By S. Resler Nelson

Quivering bud,
unfolding in the straw,
struggling to walk
on wobbly stems,
you will bloom
in the summer's warmth.

You have yet to feel
the tightening rope,
the cold, hard bit,
the closing gate.

A man must be sacrificed now and again to provide for the next generation of men.
—Amy Lowell

Men
By Sherrie J. Lyons

What is it about a distressed woman
That compels a man to make promises
That he has no intention of fulfilling
That he hopes will fade with time
And be forgotten in three months or six
But when she doesn't forget, he ignores
the gift, and the mail, and oh
why did she have to call today, his first
day back from a trip?

What is it about this distressed woman
that draws from him
sworn secrets?
The desperation in her voice?
The vehemence that drives her soul?

I do not despise you for reneging
Nor do I harbor hard feelings
For you tried and you failed
But the more important is that you tried
And I also tried and failed
So we are a pair of unlikely
bedfellows
Or perhaps we are only human

Vaquero Solitario
By Bill Lynam

I'm a vaquero, amigo.
My name is Juan Prospero.
I live down the street from
you, but you can't see me.

You look off into the hills,
The Bradshaw's, from your deck,
but you can't see the barbed-wire
and the extent of *el rancho*.

All you can see is mesquite, Alligator juniper,
Ponderosa pine, scrub, gamma grass, the silhouette of the hills.
Look closer amigo, there's a man on a horse,
he's rounding up strays, its auction time.

There're 300 head wandering the bush,
down in the ravines, not far up the slopes.
They like the draws where water ponds,
and grass grows better in the catchment.

There's a bunkhouse out there, behind the big house.
Me and two other vaqueros tend *el rancho,*
We mend fence, deliver calves,
look for sick steers, and put out licks.

We get to go home, *hogar,* once a year--
Guatemala, Mexico, San Salvador.
Mostly, we go to Western Union, that is
our peso connection to home, *hogar.*

Mi espousa y los chicos
go to the store every month—no mucho dinero.
She keeps chickens and maize and trades
with the cow farmer--milk for *los ninios.*

Mi caballo, my horse, only speaks en espanol.
He talks to me, we sing the old songs, *la concion,*
together. No giddiup, it's "hi, *arriba, arriba*"
He came with me in his trailer from home, *hogar*
He is my only love here.

Poetry is thoughts that breathe, and words that burn.
—*Thomas Gray*

Unfit
By Joe DiBuduo

I supposed you were the only one under the sun, who would rather die

than cheat or lie, but like all the others you found a way to make me

believe. Like me, you aren't worthy of love.

Even though I know that's how you are, I want to believe it's not true,

I try to accept as accurate that you'd be truthful, but I know that will never

be, because you want someone younger than me before your life is through.

I understand, and I search above and below for another too. It doesn't

matter to me, just so she's younger and prettier than you. I have a need

for love I can't have.

So, if my feelings for you were returned, you'd be spurned, and I'd soon

tire and dispose of a woman so senseless she could love a man like me.

Unlike you I'm the perfect one to avoid because I can never return what
    you feel because that's the way I am, and love isn't programmed into my
    DNA, unless it's for a dog or a cat.

I can love an animal like that, but never a woman like you for more
    than a day or two. Behind your façade you're as unfaithful as
    a Bonobo and desire whiskey and sex like a lioness in heat.

Loving you isn't worth all the pain I'd feel in the days that remain.
    My life is only a dream where someone like you is faithful to me and make
    all my pains go away, but we know that'll never be, because
    like you, for love,
    I'm unfit.

The Mole People
By Jude Crump

Under the damp clay soil live families of moles
Not for them, the arid earth of the desert
Thirty-four years living just above their burrows
Amidst forests of fir and fields thick with ferns
Never having left these places encased in fog
The valley rife with pollens and mold spores

Chronic grey cloud cover
Holding fast its coveted position
Moving ever inland to cross from the Pacific yet
Unable to scale the higher Cascades
Cities and towns trapped in dismal light

Moss encroaches ten months of the year
On roofs and the dark side of houses
Mold claims the interiors of unheated buildings
Finding no relief month after month
The dampness infiltrates aching arthritic joints
People turn inward or lash out

Cold creeps around the edges of me
Seeking entrance through the fibers of my clothing
Until neck deep in a steaming tub and slowly, slowly
The cold driven from the marrow of my bones
Leaving only flushed and wrinkled skin

Engines groaning, the plane lifts skyward
On my first flight away from moles

I see only grayness through the window

And tiny droplets skittering over windowpanes
Hopelessly blank like an empty screen
I settle back in my seat, expecting nothing more

The gray mass wicked away now
We are soaring high over a downy white quilt
The valley of green no longer visible
A spirited sun reigns over clear turquoise sky
Eyes smarting from the brilliance of it

The only home I've ever known and yet there is
The world, replete with sun drenched places
Long forgotten by valley residents with umbrellas
Awareness now settling as a soft cloak around my shoulders,
I was never intended to be one of the Mole People

"Music expresses that which cannot be put into words and that which cannot remain silent"
— *Victor Hugo*

The Conductress
By Janice Shanks

lifting her hand, fingers motion for softness
music up
strings and keys
begin her symphony
she sees beyond the things
she's seen
dreams beyond the dreams
she dreams
lifting her head, eyes in signal and approval
tones sound
brass and skins
concerto in fullness
she hears more music
than an ear can hear
she feels more rhythm
than a heart can bear
lifting her arms, batons swing the tempo
hypnotic expression
notes and chords
melody transcends us
to the places of
brightness
sadness
comfort

peace
at a crescendo
we travel back
lift our hands and hearts
the music will linger into the night
the songs will ride home with us
because the conductress
so fine tuned
orchestrated it just so

and even though it seemed
it was over
a flick of the wrist and a downward move
and the music ends
it never does

"When peoples care for you and cry for you, they can straighten out your soul."

—Langston Hughes

Funky Friend
By Dolores Comeaux-Everard

Funky Friend,
Fabulous, flamboyant, fluid.
Creativity oozes from her very fingertips,
Splashing colors, fabric, and fashion
Into designs that dazzle, daze and delight.

Funky Friend,
Hair tipped with tinsel
Nails bright deep red,
Shoes fantastic fuchsia begging an eye-
A fashion statement extraordinaire.

Funky Friend,
A Renaissance retro woman
Channels rainbow renditions
Of delight to tickle our palettes
For enlightened life and art.

Funky Friend.
Open to Divine Ideas of pleasure
Channeled from her Source of Being,
Gifting us with breathless beauty

"We love the things we love for what they are."
— *Robert Frost*

Mad House
By James Raymond Thacher

In the river below our house
A burlap bag of cats that can't
Get out shouts by in winter melt
In springtime flow as willow trees sprout
Silently from aftermath I blame the mother
And the father but not the holy ghost about
Things I want no bother with I sit and watch
Until the burlap bag floats quickly out of sight
And the sun comes out from where it was
Hiding behind a single cloud I sit here
On the porches share and after another minute
Pass on a decision to splash the boat or not
I go back into the house to beguile
All things awhile until the worst becomes forgot

"If you have the words, there's always a chance that you'll find the way."
— *Seamus Hea*ney

Maria
By Bruce Paul

She's a chili pepper hot one.
The love child of a fast gun.
For some reason, she took a fancy to me.

Her name is Maria,
And she was born to be a
Lover like no sane man has ever seen.

One night, after the bars,
In the desert, under the stars—
As free as free can be—

She was leaning on my shoulder.
That's when I told her
Everything I thought she would mean to me.

And I'd be coming back . . .
I'd be coming back
To my sweet Maria.
I'd be coming back,
And I wanted her to wait for me.

Somewhere, there's fortune.
Somewhere, there's fame,
And a man's got to do what a man's got to do.

But I've been away too long,
And things have gone all wrong.
Still, a man's got to do what a man's got to do.

And I'll be coming back . . .
I'll be coming back
To my sweet Maria.
I'll be coming back,
And I hope she's still waiting for me.

All Things Must Die
By Joe DiBuduo

You have a soul you know.
I agree and say, I have two, not one
and point to the bottom of my shoes.
Not those soles you fool echoes intimately inside my skull.
A fist grips my heart and the beat suddenly stops.
Now that you're dead, you can see where your soul resides
echoes throughout my corpse with a still functioning brain.

I know, but why do I have to go long before I want,
and when I do, where will I go?

Is there really pie in the sky?

It has been said, life is better after death, but I want to live
while I'm alive, to put ice cream on my pie and have one
more chance to have sex.
I search through all my body parts, but there is no soul
to be found. I'm a soulless man," I cry to the skies above.
When you don't believe in me, that's the price you pay, the
crashing voice resonates throughout my dead body, causing it
to move. Unfair, unfair, my lifeless form declares.
Tell me which God you are? Are you Achtland, the Celtic
Goddess of wanton love?"
Love is a word falsely attributed to me. If I loved, would your
world be such a mess?" the voice assumed I understood.
Tell me then, are you be Xtabay, the Mayan Goddess of
Seduction
without love in your heart?

Or are you an evil being who made me and the rest of
humanity so
you'd have someone with whom to play?"
For a soulless man you should be begging for clemency
instead
of questioning me.

You must be the Son of perdition," I exclaim. The antichrist,
the deceiver, chief of demons, Beelzebub, the father of lies.
Laughter shook the entire sky and I got a preview of my soul
being
carried away by birds of prey. Wait! I cry, I see my soul.
Laughter shook the sky and the Earth. Too late my boy,
it's gone now and will never return. You're doomed to the
bottomless pit for eternity since you didn't know my name.
One more chance, I cry and see dark clouds fluctuating
throughout the darkening sky, merging into an image of a
terrifying old man with an unpleasant face.

The mouth made of clouds opens and releases crashing
thunder
clearing all other clouds from the sky. You'll never have
another
chance, I'll see to that, booms round the heavens.
I gather all the electro-mechanical energy within my brain's
limbic system and send it to my amygdala to project my
thoughts onto the only cloud left in the sky, causing it to burst.
Screams fill the air as my mental powers disintegrate the God
who has made me and all others.

He should have known, because he made the rule, all things
must die.

*"We cannot tell the precise moment when friendship is formed.
As in filling a vessel drop by drop, there is at last a drop which
makes it run over; so in a series of kindnesses there is at last one
which makes the heart run over."*
—Ray Bradbury

Sherrie J. Lyons
So long, Tami

So long as you are alive
I want to be part of your life:
To chat with you over the phone
To sit with you alone—or not—
In a car or at a restaurant
At my house or at a park
Anywhere your spark
Flames or flickers or faintly glows
Because my heart knows
That your life fuels my life.

The smile in your voice brightens my day
Your sunny spirit shows me a way
To live my life better
And whether or not I achieve this end
I can't thank you enough for being my friend
For so long, Tami—forty years or more—
And no matter what life holds in store
I'll always feel blessed
Because you possess
A warmth that can't pass away.

*Dedicated to Tami Knapp (1959-2017)

Love is a friendship set to music—Joseph Campbell

Heartbroken
By Bruce Paul

Who gets lost in romance,
After the wine and the candlelight
And the last slow dance?
Who gets lost in romance?
It breaks my heart to think about it,
But I've been heartbroken before.

And who gets hurt in love,
After the last sacrifice
And the last flight of the dove?
Who gets hurt in love?
It breaks my heart to think about it,
But I've been heartbroken before.

Disappointment and betrayal—
Turmoil at every turn.
We study every detail,
But do we ever learn?
Do we ever learn?

And who gets killed in war?
Christians, Muslims, and Jews.
Is there any hope anymore?
Tell me, who gets killed in war?
It breaks my heart to think about it,
But I've been heartbroken before.

'Publishing a volume of verse is like dropping a rose-petal down the Grand Canyon and waiting for the echo.'—Don Marquis

Summer Memories
By Pat Fogarty

Cotton candy
At the beach
Saltwater
On your feet

Boardwalk splinters
Walk with care
Vendors hawk
Everywhere

Roller coasters
Often fly
Funhouse mirrors
Always lie

Guess your weight
Two hoops win
Frozen custard
On your chin

Kites and birds
Fill the air
Spandex males
Folding chairs

Dainty ladies
Seeking shade
Younger men
Surfing waves

Sandy children
Splash and play
Crafted castles
Melt away

Ocean tides
Rise and fall
Summer memories
Some recall

Great is the art of beginning, but greater is the art of ending.

—Henry Wadsworth Longfellow